A Critical Analysis of Critical Loss Analysis

Daniel P. O'Brien and Abraham L. Wickelgren[*]

May 23, 2003

Abstract

Critical loss analysis is often used to argue that firms with large margins have more to lose from a reduction in sales and hence are less likely to increase prices. This argument ignores the implication of economic theory that profit-maximizing competitors that do not coordinate their pricing only have large margins if their customers are not very price sensitive. We explore the implications of critical loss analysis using an internally consistent model of oligopoly. We show that for a given degree of substitutability between the merging firms' products, firms with larger pre-merger margins will raise prices more than firms with smaller margins. This reinforces the traditional view that mergers are more likely to harm consumers when the merging firms have greater market power, as measured by their margins. We also derive internally consistent formulas for evaluating the profitability of price increases when defining markets and evaluating unilateral competitive effects.

I. Introduction

Critical loss analysis is a widely-used technique in antitrust practice.[1] The basic idea is simple. One asks: "given a price increase of X percent,[2] what would the percentage loss in unit sales have to be to make the price increase unprofitable?" This loss is referred to as the "critical loss for an X-percent price increase." If the actual loss is less than the critical loss, the price

---

[*] The authors are economists at the U.S. Federal Trade Commission. Patrick DeGraba, Alan Frankel, Ezra Friedman, Jerry Hausman, Stephen Holland, Dan Hosken, David Scheffman, David Schmidt, Carl Shapiro, Mike Vita and Charlotte Wojcik provided many useful comments and suggestions. The views in this article are those of the authors and do not necessarily reflect those of the Federal Trade Commission or any individual Commissioner.

[1] The use of critical loss analysis was first suggested by Barry C. Harris and Joseph J. Simons, "Focusing Market Definition: How Much Substitution is Necessary?" *Research in Law and Economics*, v. 12, 1989, p.207-226. Since it was proposed, it has appeared in numerous White Papers presented to the antitrust agencies, numerous pre-trial affidavits, and expert testimony offered on behalf of antitrust defendants.

[2] The analysis applies equally well for any potential price increase.

increase would pay. Otherwise it would not.

The most common uses of critical loss analysis are to define relevant markets and assess the competitive effects of mergers. For example, experts representing merging parties often use this technique to argue that where margins are high, the product market must be broader than the government contends. The argument is that the larger are the margins, the greater is the reduction in profits from sales lost after a price increase. Therefore, it takes a smaller critical loss to make a given price increase by a hypothetical monopolist unprofitable. The experts then argue that the actual loss from a 5 percent price increase would surely exceed the critical loss, implying that the relevant market must include substitutes that are not included in the government's alleged market.[3]

Similar logic is often used to argue that a merged firm would not have an incentive to increase price by a given amount following a merger. Again, the argument is that the larger is the merging firm's margin, the less likely it is that a given price increase would be profitable.

Critical loss analysis is simple and has a degree of intuitive appeal. Unfortunately, the standard way that critical loss analysis is applied (henceforth, "standard critical loss analysis") ignores two key points, often leading to inconsistent logic and erroneous conclusions. First, standard critical loss analysis fails to recognize that a firm's margin provides information about the magnitude of the sales it is likely to lose from a price increase. If pre-merger prices are chosen to maximize profits, higher margins typically imply that customers are not very price sensitive (otherwise, a firm could substantially increase its sales by making a small price cut,

---

[3] The FTC/DOJ Merger Guidelines define a product market as the narrowest set of products such that a hypothetical profit-maximizing monopolist would raise price a small but significant amount. U.S. Dep't of Justice and Federal Trade Comm'n, Horizontal Merger Guidelines, §1.1 (1992, rev. 1997). For a discussion of the use of demand elasticities in defining antitrust markets, See Werden, Gregory, "Demand Elasticities in Antitrust Analysis," *Antitrust Law Journal*, 66, 363, 1998.

which would imply that the current price is not profit-maximizing).[4] This means that when margins are larger, a price increase will usually result in *fewer* lost sales than when margins are smaller. In short, the argument that a large percentage of sales would be lost in the event of a price increase is typically inconsistent with the existence of large pre-merger margins for profit maximizing firms.

A second fundamental error of the standard critical loss analysis is that it ignores the importance of the degree of substitutability (e.g., the cross elasticities of demand or diversion ratios) among the products of the firm considering the price increase. The greater the cross elasticities, the more the firm will profit from increasing the price of one product because it will capture a larger percentage of the lost sales through increases in the sales of its other products. As an extreme example, consider a merger that would combine two products that have zero or very low cross elasticities between each other. A post-merger price increase on one of the products would not significantly raise the sales of the other, so the merger provides little or no incentive to raise price. On the other hand, suppose the merging firms have very high cross elasticities between each other. In this case, a price increase for one of the merging products results in substantial sales diverted to the other product, increasing the merged firm's profits. If margins are high, so that the diverted sales are highly profitable, the merged firm will have a relatively higher incentive to raise price absent offsetting entry, product repositioning, or efficiency gains.

In the "hypothetical monopolist test" outlined in the Merger Guidelines for defining markets, the hypothetical monopolist always controls multiple products. The question of whether a price increase would be profitable *cannot* be answered without accounting for the

---

[4] This assumes that the firms are not coordinating their behavior. If the firms are tacitly colluding, then margins could be large even when each firm's own demand is fairly elastic.

cross elasticities among the products under the monopolist's control. Similarly, since a merger alters the set of products under a firm's control, the analyst *must* account for cross elasticities when assessing the profitability of a post-merger price increase. However, critical loss analysts often fail to do this.

The important roles of the margin/elasticity relationship and cross elasticities for optimal pricing are stressed in economics and business school courses on pricing and strategy. However, the implications of these factors for critical loss analysis are not widely appreciated in the antitrust community. The purpose of this article is to clarify the role of these factors in firms' pricing decisions and to explore rigorously the implications of these factors for critical loss analysis.[5]

We examine critical loss analysis using a standard Bertrand pricing model, which is the most widely-used framework in economics for modeling oligopoly among price-setting firms that do not coordinate their behavior. We focus on differentiated products, although the central result that high margins tend to make post-merger price increases more likely also emerges from standard theories of competition among producers of homogenous products.[6] The analysis is applicable both to market definition, where the merger would be a hypothetical merger to monopoly, and competitive effects analysis, where the question is whether it would be profitable for the merging firms to increase price after the merger. By explicitly modeling oligopoly price-

---

[5] We should note that our critique does not invalidate the critical loss *formula* derived in Harris and Simons (op. cit.) as an algebraic statement about the loss necessary to make a given price increase unprofitable. Our criticism is directed at the application of the formula without regard to whether the assumptions and conclusions in the application are consistent with standard economic theory.

[6] If the products in the industry are homogenous, then large margins are often associated with capacity constraints. In this case, the fringe supply elasticity plays a role analogous to cross elasticities, i.e., it affects the amount of substitution away from the hypothetical monopolist (or the merging firms) in the event of a price increase or quantity decrease. Thus, the profitability of a price increase depends in part on the elasticity of the fringe supply.

setting and carrying out an internally consistent analysis within this framework, we obtain the following results: (1) For a given degree of product substitutability between the products (that is, a given cross-price elasticity or diversion ratio), larger margins make it *less* likely that the actual loss will exceed the critical loss from a price increase.[7] (2) Under linear and constant elasticity demand, simple conditions determine when the actual loss from a price increase will exceed the critical loss. These conditions require estimation of the cross-price elasticities (or diversion ratios) between the products of the merging parties, in addition to the merging firms' margins. An implication for antitrust practice is that testimony about the demand curve is most helpful when it focuses on the substitutability (cross-price elasticities or diversion ratios) between the merging products.[8]

Since critical loss analysis has become such a widely used tool, our criticism might be viewed skeptically by antitrust practitioners. In anticipation of this skepticism, we want to state up front the assumptions that underlie our key results. Our most important result is that higher margins typically make it *more* likely that a price increase by merging firms will be profitable. This result requires four main assumptions: (1) firms attempt to maximize profits before and after the merger; (2) the merger enhances the degree of coordination between the merging firms' products; (3) the response of consumers to a small price increase is not significantly greater than their response to a small price decrease; and (4) the cost of a small increase in output is not

---

[7] Of course, high margins probably mean that cross-price elasticities are not too large; the point is that one needs to know both own- and cross-price elasticities.

[8] Other authors have noted the pitfalls that can arise if critical loss analysis is not applied within a consistent economic framework. In a recent article that we learned about while this article was being reviewed, Michael Katz and Carl Shapiro present a critique that makes many of the same points that we make here. See Katz, Michael and Carl Shapiro, "Critical Loss: Let's Tell the Whole Story," forthcoming in *Antitrust Magazine.* See also Langenfeld James and Wenquing Li, "Critical Loss Analysis in Evaluating Mergers," *The Antitrust Bulletin*, Summer 2001, pp. 299-337; Danger, Kenneth L. and H.E. Frech III, "Critical Thinking about `Critical Loss' in Antitrust," *The Antitrust Bulletin*, Summer 2001, pp. 339-355, and Werden, Gregory J., "Beyond Critical Loss: Tailoring Applications of the

significantly greater than the cost savings from a small reduction in output.

Assumptions 1 and 2 are core premises of competition policy toward horizontal mergers. The assumption that profit maximization "provides a good first approximation in describing business behavior"[9] is a basic postulate of most of economic analysis. Profit maximization is also a key assumption of critical loss analysis, which involves balancing the gains and losses from a price increase. The assumption that mergers make coordination more likely may not hold in some cases if firms have discovered ways to coordinate without merging. However, even in these cases, coordination has a chance to break down if the firms are kept separate but will not break down if they merge.

Assumptions 3 and 4 amount to assuming away "kinks" in the firms' demand and cost curves, so that the responsiveness of each curve to a small increase in price is similar to the responsiveness to a small price decrease. Economic theory does not rule out such kinks. Economists usually assume that cost and demand curves are smooth rather than kinked, in part because this simplifies the analysis, but also because this assumption is usually reasonable for broad ranges of prices and quantities. For example, if the products in question have many heterogeneous customers, then aggregate demand curves will be relatively smooth. Similarly, if the inputs used in production (labor, supplies, capital equipment) are scaleable, then cost curves will be smooth as well. Competition policy is built partly on presumptions that flow from economic analysis, and our view is that Assumptions 3 and 4 are the "normal" cases appropriate for establishing such presumptions. Of course, if credible evidence that these assumptions are

---

Hypothetical Monopolist Paradigm," mimeo, U.S. Department of Justice, Antitrust Division, Economic Analysis Group, July 2002.

[9] Scherer, F.M. *Industrial Markett Structure and Economic Performance*, 2nd ed., Chicago: Rand-McNally, 1980, p. 41.

violated presents itself, it should be incorporated into the analysis of the effects of a merger. We discuss some ways that these assumptions may be violated in Section III.B.

In our formal analysis we make additional assumptions both for expositional purposes and to derive formulas for specific cases. Our formulas assume constant marginal cost, just as standard critical loss analysis does. We present formulas that apply only to the special cases of symmetric Bertrand competition and linear or constant elasticity demand. However, one could obtain similar qualitative results (but different formulas) under different assumptions about the nature of rivalry, demand and costs. While cross elasticities play a key role under differentiated Bertrand competition, the elasticity of fringe supply becomes important under quantity competition with homogenous products (either Cournot competition, or competition between a dominant firm and a competitive fringe). Different assumptions about demand and costs would affect the quantitative analysis but would not affect our main conclusions.

The remainder of this article is organized as follows. Section II presents the standard critical loss analysis for a hypothetical merger. Section III evaluates the standard critical loss analysis using elementary economic theory and shows how to modify the analysis to make it internally consistent. Section IV discusses two recent antitrust cases in which the standard critical loss analysis was applied and shows how the conclusions change if an internally consistent approach is used. Section V concludes with a discussion of the role of critical loss analysis in antitrust practice.

II. The Standard Critical Loss Analysis – A Typical Example

For the sake of discussion, imagine two symmetric firms, A and B, each selling a single differentiated product in competition with several other firms.[10] To simplify the analysis, we assume linear demand and constant marginal cost. We also assume that each firm chooses its own price unilaterally to maximize profits prior to the merger.

Suppose firms A and B propose to merge. The government believes that the appropriate product market for analyzing the merger includes only products A and B. The merging firms contend that the market is broader. In support of their claim, the merging firms' consultants present a standard critical loss analysis. They argue as follows:

> The percentage margin earned by firms A and B is 60 percent. Thus, the "critical loss" in unit sales above which a 5 percent price increase would be unprofitable is 7.7 percent. The testimony indicates that a 5-percent increase in the prices of products A and B would likely result in a loss in unit sales of A and B of at least 10 percent, which exceeds the critical loss. This means that a 5 percent price increase would not be profitable, so the relevant product market must include other products in addition to products A and B.

This argument is typical of the critical loss analyses presented in numerous antitrust cases. In order to evaluate it, we first need to understand how the critical loss is determined.

The critical loss for an X-percent price increase is the percentage reduction in quantity required for the price increase to leave profits unchanged.[11] Calculating the critical loss requires balancing two effects: 1) a given price increase raises the profit margin earned on all units that are sold, but 2) it also reduces the quantity demanded resulting in fewer units being sold. The critical loss is the percentage reduction in quantity such that these two effects just balance. If the

---

[10] By symmetric we mean that firms A and B have the same cost functions and symmetric, but potentially differentiated, demand. Symmetric demand means that the firms will sell same amount if they charge the same prices, and that firm A's demand at one pair of prices is the same as what firm B's demand would be if their prices were interchanged.

[11] The 1992 Merger Guidelines define markets by asking whether a *profit-maximizing* monopolist would impose a "small but significant and non-transitory price increase" (SSNIP). The critical loss calculation, by contrast, addresses the question of whether a particular SSNIP, not necessarily the profit-maximizing one, yields higher profit than the pre-merger price. A rough approximation (exact for linear demand) is that the profit-maximizing price increase is half as much as the price increase that leaves profits unchanged. For example, a 5 percent price increase would be optimal (approximately) if a 10 percent price increase leaves profits unchanged.

reduction in unit sales is greater than the critical loss, then the price increase will reduce profits. If the reduction in unit sales is less then the critical loss, the price increase will increase profits.

A small amount of notation is useful to describe this calculation. Suppose that firms A and B both produce at constant unit cost c. The pre-merger price of products A and B is p, and the pre-merger total quantity of A and B is q. Denote a given price increase for both products A and B by Δp and the resulting change in the total quantity of A and B by Δq. Since the quantity demanded falls with price, the change in quantity, Δq, is a negative number.

With this notation, the critical loss calculation is easy to describe. The benefit to the hypothetical monopolist from a price increase is the amount of the price increase times the quantity that will be sold at the new price, i.e., $\Delta p[q+\Delta q]$. The cost to monopolist of the price increase is equal to the pre-merger margin times the quantity reduction caused by the price increase, i.e., $-(p-c)\Delta q$. The benefit and cost of the price increase just balance if

$$(1) \quad \left(\begin{array}{c}\text{Benefit of} \\ \text{price increase}\end{array}\right) = \Delta p[q+\Delta q] = -(p-c)\Delta q = \left(\begin{array}{c}\text{Cost of} \\ \text{price increase}\end{array}\right).$$

The formula for the critical loss is found by dividing both sides of this equation by pq. This gives

$$(2) \quad \frac{\Delta p}{p}\left[1+\frac{\Delta q}{q}\right] = -\left(\frac{p-c}{p}\right)\frac{\Delta q}{q}.$$

The critical loss is the percentage reduction in quantity, $-\Delta q/q$, that satisfies condition (2).[12] Solving for the critical loss gives

$$(3) \quad -\frac{\Delta q}{q} = \text{Critical Loss} = \frac{\Delta p/p}{\Delta p/p + m}$$

---

[12] Throughout the article we associate percentages with decimal equivalents. For example, if $\Delta q/q = .10$, the percentage reduction in quantity would be 10 percent.

where $m = (p-c)/p$ is the margin measured as a percentage of the price. Since $\Delta p/p$ is just the percentage price increase, condition (3) implies that the critical loss for an X-percent price increase is

$$(4) \qquad \textit{Critical Loss} = \frac{X}{X+m}.$$

The formula for the critical loss in (4) shows that for a given price increase of X percent, the critical loss is smaller the larger is the margin. Intuitively, the larger is the margin, the greater the profit lost from a given reduction in quantity, so the smaller the reduction in quantity required for a given price increase to be unprofitable.

If the margin is 60 percent, as the merging firms in our example contend, the critical loss from a 5 percent price increase is

$$(5) \qquad \textit{Critical Loss} = \frac{.05}{.05+.6} \cong .077,$$

or about 7.7 percent. In the example, the merging firms argue that the unit sales lost from a 5 percent price increase on both products would be at least 10 percent. Since this loss exceeds the critical loss, they conclude that a 5 percent price increase would not be profitable. The implication they draw is that the price increase would cause enough customers to switch to other products that the price increase would be unprofitable, suggesting that the relevant market must include other products in addition to products A and B.

III. Economics of Critical Loss

A. Inconsistency of the Standard Critical Loss Analysis

We will now analyze the merging firms' argument using standard economic theory. At the outset, we should note there is nothing wrong with the standard critical loss *calculation* itself.

The calculation is simply algebra, and formula (4) is certainly correct. The problem arises in the interpretation of (4) in light of evidence about the actual loss from a given price increase. Economic theory tells us quite a bit about the relationship between the actual loss from a price increase and the critical loss expressed in (4). An antitrust argument that is grounded in economics must recognize this relationship when evaluating evidence about the actual loss from a price increase. We will show that, by ignoring this relationship, the standard critical loss analysis is internally inconsistent and often leads to faulty conclusions.

We begin our critique by describing what economic theory tells us about the actual loss in unit sales from a given price increase. It is helpful conceptually to think about breaking the price increase into two steps involving first an increase in the price of product A and then an equivalent increase in the price of product B.[13] A price increase of X percent for product A causes a reduction in the quantity demanded for product A. Because products A and B are substitutes, it also causes an increase in the demand for product B. Denote the own elasticity of demand for product A as E^{Own} and the cross elasticity of demand for product B with respect to the price of product A as E^{Cross}.[14] An X-percent increase in the price of product A causes the unit sales of product A to fall by the amount of the price increase times the own elasticity of demand,

---

[13] If the firms have multiple products, then one needs to consider how increases in the prices of each product affect the demand for all of the products of both firms. The analysis is similar, though more complex, and the qualitative conclusions for critical loss analysis are unchanged.

[14] The own elasticity of demand for product A is the percentage reduction in unit sales for product A divided by the percentage increase in its price for a small increase in price. The cross elasticity of demand for product B with respect to the price of product A is the percentage increase in unit sales for product B divided by the percentage increase in the price of product A for a small increase in price. We follow the convention of expressing own elasticities as positive numbers even though the change in own quantity from a price increase is negative. Technically, these definitions are for "point" elasticities corresponding to small price changes, which generally may differ from "arc" elasticities appropriate for evaluating the effects of larger price increases like those contemplated by the merger guidelines (e.g., 5 and 10 percent). While arc elasticities are usually defined using the average price and quantity as the base, we use the initial price and quantity as the base since the merger guidelines measure percentage price increases using initial prices as the base. With arc elasticities defined this way, the point and arc elasticities are equivalent under the special case of linear demand.

i.e., by XE^{Own} percent. Similarly, the price increase causes the unit sales of product B to rise by the amount of the price increase times the cross elasticity of demand, or XE^{Cross} percent. Since products A and B are symmetric in this example, an X-percent increase in the price of product B causes the unit sales of product B to fall by XE^{Own} percent and the unit sales of product A to rise by XE^{Cross} percent. Combining these effects, a price increase of X percent for both products A and B causes a reduction in the unit sales of $X[E^{Own} - E^{Cross}]$ percent for both products. So the actual loss in percentage terms experienced by the hypothetical monopolist from an X-percent price increase is

$$(6) \qquad Actual\ Loss = X[E^{Own} - E^{Cross}].\ [15]$$

One more step is necessary before we can assess the consistency of standard critical loss analysis. The pre-merger margins of firms A and B provide information about the extent to which consumers are willing to substitute away from their products. A profit maximizing firm raises price to the level at which the benefit of an additional price increase on each unit sold is just offset by the reduction in sales due to the additional price increase. Denote the quantity of product A by q^A, the increase in the price of product A by Δp^A, and the associated change in the quantity of product A by Δq^A (note that Δq^A is negative). Profit maximization requires that firm A raise price to the point where the gains from an additional price increase, $\Delta p^A [q^A + \Delta q^A]$, just offset the cost of the price increase, $-(p-c)\Delta q^A$. That is

$$(7) \qquad \begin{pmatrix} Benefit\ of \\ price\ increase \end{pmatrix} = \Delta p^A [q^A + \Delta q^A] = -(p^A - c)\Delta q^A = \begin{pmatrix} Cost\ of \\ price\ increase \end{pmatrix}.$$

Note that the profit maximization condition (7) is the same type of balancing condition as that

---

[15] Adding the percentage changes in own and cross effects this way is permitted by the assumption that products A and B are symmetric. The intuition for the inconsistency in standard critical loss analysis in the symmetric case carries over to the asymmetric case.

used in the critical loss equation (1), except that it must hold for each firm individually. If we divide both sides of (7) by $q^A \Delta p^A / p^A$, the condition can be rewritten as

$$(8) \qquad m = \frac{1}{E^{Own}}\left[1 + \frac{\Delta q^A}{q^A}\right]$$

where $E^{Own} = -(\Delta q^A/q^A)/(\Delta p^A/p^A)$ is the own-elasticity of demand for product A. If firm A is maximizing its profits, the balancing condition (8) must hold for an arbitrarily small increase in price. For a small price increase, Δq^A is approximately zero. So the profit maximization condition boils down to

$$(9) \qquad m = \frac{1}{E^{Own}}.$$

Condition (9) is just the inverse elasticity rule for profit maximization familiar from elementary microeconomic theory. It is derived from the same type of balancing condition as that used to derive the critical loss. Since the calculations are so similar, it should not be surprising that the assumption of profit maximization has strong implications for critical loss analysis, as we now show.

Substituting (9) into (6), the actual loss experienced by the hypothetical monopolist from an X-percent price increase is

$$(10) \qquad Actual\ Loss = X\left[\frac{1}{m} - E^{Cross}\right].^{16}$$

We can use condition (10) to evaluate the merging firms' critical loss analysis in our example. A price increase of X percent for products A and B will be unprofitable if the actual loss exceeds the critical loss, that is, if

---

[16] Again, because the point and arc elasticities are equal under linear demand, we can use the relationship between the margin and the point elasticity to substitute for the arc elasticity of demand.

$$(11) \quad \text{Actual Loss} = X\left[\frac{1}{m} - E^{Cross}\right] > \frac{X}{X+m} = \text{Critical Loss}$$

After a bit of algebra, we find that the actual loss exceeds the critical loss if and only if

$$(12) \quad \frac{X}{m(X+m)} = \frac{\text{Critical Loss}}{m} > E^{Cross}.$$

Notice that the left-hand-side of condition (12) falls as the margin increases. This implies the following important result: **holding cross elasticities between the merging firms constant, a given price increase is *more* likely to be profitable the larger is the margin.**[17] This implication of standard microeconomic theory is exactly the opposite of that implied by the standard critical loss analysis, though it is completely in line with the conventional wisdom that mergers tend to be more problematic in more concentrated industries.

An equivalent way to express condition (12) that is sometimes easier to interpret is in terms of the diversion ratio between A and B, which is the fraction of sales lost by A when it raises price that are recaptured by B.[18] Under symmetry, the cross elasticity is equal to the diversion ratio divided by the margin. Substituting this relationship into condition (12), we have that (with symmetric demand) a price increase is unprofitable if and only if

$$(13) \quad \frac{X}{(X+m)} = \text{Critical Loss} > \text{Diversion Ratio}.$$

---

[17] Technical readers may wonder what implicit assumptions are being made about other cross elasticities in making this statement. To be precise, suppose consumers buy three products: A, B, and C. Denote the elasticity (or cross elasticity) of demand for product i with respect to the price of product j as E_{ij}, and denote the consumers' budget share of product i as s_i. The microeconomic theory of the consumer implies that budget shares and elasticities are related according to the equation $(1-E_{AA})s_A + E_{BA} s_B + E_{CA} s_C = 0$. This implies that for any given cross elasticity E_{BA}, a lower value of E_{AA} (a higher margin) is associated with a smaller cross elasticity between products C and A and/or a larger budget share for product A.

[18] Formally, the diversion ratio from A to B can be defined as $D=(q^B/q^A)(E^{Cross}/E^{Own})$. See Shapiro, Carl, "Mergers with Differentiated Products," *Antitrust Magazine*, Spring 1996, p. 23-30. Using this definition and the margin elasticity relationship $m=1/E^{Own}$, it is straightforward to translate the cross elasticity condition into the diversion ratio condition presented in the text.

Recall that the merging firms in our example argued that the actual loss from a 5 percent price increase for both products would be 10 percent or more. However, if we accept the merging firms' assumption that the margin is 60 percent, condition (10) implies that the actual loss is

$$(14) \quad Actual\ Loss = .05\left[\frac{1}{.6} - E^{Cross}\right]$$

$$= .083 - .05 E^{Cross}$$

$$< .083,$$

or less than 8.3 percent.[19] We conclude that if firms A and B were pricing unilaterally to maximize their own profits prior to the proposed merger, and if the margin is correctly measured,[20] then the actual loss from a 5 percent price increase *could not be* as high as the merging firms contend.

This logical error appears repeatedly in the standard critical loss analysis. The key mistake is the failure to recognize that margins will be high *only if* customers are not very sensitive to changes in price, i.e., only if the actual loss from an additional price increase would be small. We know this from the margin elasticity relationship implied by the assumption of profit maximization, $m=1/E^{Own}$, or $E^{Own}=1/m$. This condition implies that the actual loss from a price increase by an individual firm varies inversely with the margin. The actual loss for the hypothetical monopolist must be smaller than the loss for an individual firm because some of the lost sales are recaptured through increased sales of substitute products. For a given cross elasticity between products A and B, the recapture rate is independent of the margin. Therefore,

---

[19] The last inequality in (14) is true because the cross elasticity is positive for substitute goods.

[20] We assume throughout this analysis that margins are appropriately measured, as this is a necessary condition for critical loss analysis to be valid. Of course, an inconsistency between the actual loss and the margin could be attributable to an error in either number.

the actual loss that a hypothetical monopolist experiences from a given price increase is also smaller the larger is the margin.

In our example, the actual loss to the hypothetical monopolist from a 5 percent price increase cannot exceed 8.3 percent. This is the actual loss when the cross elasticity between products A and B is zero (to see this, set $E^{Cross}=0$ in (14)). Note that this amount is greater than the critical loss of 7.7 percent in the example, so that it is still possible for the actual loss to exceed the critical loss and for the *conclusions* of the critical loss analysis to be correct. However, the actual loss exceeds the critical loss in the example only if the cross elasticity is quite small, i.e., only if

$$(15) \qquad Actual\ Loss = .05[\frac{1}{.6} - E^{Cross}] > \frac{.05}{.05 + .6} = Critical\ Loss.$$

Condition (15) is true only if $E^{Cross} < .13$. This is a fairly low cross elasticity, indicating that products A and B are not especially close substitutes. For example, the diversion ratio from A to B would have to be less than 8 percent. Again, this is in line with standard intuition: in a concentrated industry with high margins and significant diversion ratios, a merger is likely to be anticompetitive in the absence of offsetting efficiencies, entry, or product repositioning.

Although the discussion to this point has focused on the effects of combining two products, it should be apparent that the analysis extends straightforwardly to the effects of combining any number of symmetric products. In particular, an X-percent price increase for N symmetric products is profitable if the *sum* of the cross elasticities between any one of the N products and the N-1 rival products in the group exceeds the critical cross elasticity, or if the *sum* of the diversion ratios exceeds the critical diversion ratio.[21] Formulas 6 through 15 are still valid,

---

[21] The analog of equation (6) for the N-product case is $Actual\ Loss = X[E^{Own} - (N-1)E^{Cross}]$. The sum of the diversion ratios from one product to the other N-1 products is the "aggregate diversion ratio" defined by Katz and

but the cross elasticity E^{Cross} is interpreted as the sum of the cross elasticities between one of the products and the other products in the group. Similarly, the diversion ratio is interpreted as the "aggregate diversion ratio" from one product to all the others in the group. Using this interpretation, it is possible to use conditions (12) and (13) to conduct the hypothetical monopolist test for more than two products. The formulas are exact when products are symmetric. A more complex calculation is required for asymmetric cases. However, a conservative lower bound on the critical cross elasticity and diversion ratio can be found by using the smallest margin of all the products in the group to evaluate the formulas.

Table 1 presents the critical cross elasticities and critical diversion ratios below which a price increase for a group of products is unprofitable given different pre-merger margins. Referring to our earlier example in which the margin was 60 percent, the table shows that a 5 percent price increase by a hypothetical monopolist of N products would be unprofitable if the sum of the cross elasticities between one of the products and the other products in the group is less than .13, or if the aggregate diversion ratio (the sum of the diversion ratios from one product to the others in the group) is less than 7.7 percent. More generally, Table 1 shows that the critical cross elasticity and diversion ratio is smaller the higher is the margin, which is the main point of this article.

Shapiro, op. cit. Condition (13) shows that a particular price increase will be unprofitable if the aggregate diversion ratio is less then the critical loss, as Katz and Shapiro emphasize in their article.

Table 1: Critical Cross Elasticities and Diversion Ratios for the Profitability of an Increase in the Price of N Symmetric Products – Linear Demand

Margin	1% Price Increase		5% Price Increase		10% Price Increase	
	Critical Cross Elasticity	Critical Diversion Ratio	Critical Cross Elasticity	Critical Diversion Ratio	Critical Cross Elasticity	Critical Diversion Ratio
10%	0.91	9.1%	3.33	33.3%	5.00	50.0%
15%	0.42	6.3%	1.67	25.0%	2.67	40.0%
20%	0.24	4.8%	1.00	20.0%	1.67	33.3%
25%	0.15	3.8%	0.67	16.7%	1.14	28.6%
30%	0.11	3.2%	0.48	14.3%	0.83	25.0%
35%	0.08	2.8%	0.36	12.5%	0.63	22.2%
40%	0.06	2.4%	0.28	11.1%	0.50	20.0%
45%	0.05	2.2%	0.22	10.0%	0.40	18.2%
50%	0.04	2.0%	0.18	9.1%	0.33	16.7%
55%	0.03	1.8%	0.15	8.3%	0.28	15.4%
60%	0.03	1.6%	0.13	7.7%	0.24	14.3%
65%	0.02	1.5%	0.11	7.1%	0.21	13.3%
70%	0.02	1.4%	0.10	6.7%	0.18	12.5%
75%	0.02	1.3%	0.08	6.3%	0.16	11.8%
80%	0.02	1.2%	0.07	5.9%	0.14	11.1%
85%	0.01	1.2%	0.07	5.6%	0.12	10.5%
90%	0.01	1.1%	0.06	5.3%	0.11	10.0%

Note: For a price increase on N ≥ 2 products, the critical cross elasticity (critical diversion ratio) is compared with the sum of the cross elasticities (diversion ratios) between one product and each of the N-1 other products in the group.

The critical cross elasticities and diversion ratios in Table 1 are applicable for the special case of linear (i.e., "straight line") demand. Linear demand has the property that as the price increases, the own elasticity of demand rises, gradually dampening incentives for further price increases. It is worth pointing out that for many other demand curves used by antitrust economists (constant elasticity, logit, AIDS, semi-log), the elasticity does not rise as sharply with price as it does with linear demand. This means that the critical cross elasticity and diversion ratios are typically smaller under these other demand assumptions than they are for linear demand.

Another important special case is constant elasticity demand, which assumes that the elasticity does not change with price. Table 2 presents the critical cross elasticities and diversion ratios for the constant elasticity case.[22] The critical values are significantly lower in this case than they are under linear demand. This difference arises because the actual loss from a given price increase is smaller under constant elasticity demand than it is for linear demand given the same initial own-price elasticity. As for the case of linear demand, the critical cross elasticity and diversion ratio fall as the margin rises. This confirms our main point that a merger is more likely to result in higher prices the higher is the pre-merger margin.

---

[22] We explain here how the critical values in Table 2 were generated. For constant elasticity demand, unlike linear demand, point and arc elasticities are different. The constant (point) elasticity demand curve is $q = ap_1^{-E^{Own}} p_2^{E^{Cross}}$. The arc own elasticity (in absolute value) is the percentage reduction in quantity divided by the percentage increase in price. This is given by the following formula:

$$arcE^{Own} = -\frac{a((1+X)p_1)^{-E^{Own}} p_2^{E^{Cross}} - ap_1^{-E^{Own}} p_2^{E^{Cross}}}{X(ap_1^{-E^{Own}} p_2^{E^{Cross}})}$$

Simplifying and imposing symmetry, this can be rewritten as follows:

$$arcE^{Own} = \frac{1-(1+X)^{-E^{Own}}}{X} \neq E^{Own}$$

A similar calculation yields the arc cross elasticity:

$$arcE^{Cross} = \frac{(1+X)^{E^{Cross}} - 1}{X} \neq E^{Cross}$$

We can use the arc elasticities to rewrite the actual loss, equation (6), in terms of the point elasticities.

$$ActualLoss = 2 - (1+X)^{-E^{Own}} - (1+X)^{E^{Cross}}$$

Because profit maximization implies that the margin is the inverse of the own point elasticity, we can write the actual loss as follows:

$$ActualLoss = 2 - (1+X)^{-1/m} - (1+X)^{E^{Cross}}$$

Equating the actual loss with the Critical Loss, $X/(X+m)$, and solving for E^{Cross}, we find that the Actual Loss exceeds the Critical Loss if and only if:

$$E^{Cross} < \frac{\ln(2 - (1+X)^{-1/m} - \frac{X}{X+m})}{\ln(1+X)}$$

This is the formula used to generate Table 2.

Table 2: Critical Cross Elasticities and Diversion Ratios for the Profitability of an Increase in the Price of N Symmetric Products – Constant Elasticity Demand

Margin	1% Price Increase		5% Price Increase		10% Price Increase	
	Critical Cross Elasticity	Critical Diversion Ratio	Critical Cross Elasticity	Critical Diversion Ratio	Critical Cross Elasticity	Critical Diversion Ratio
10%	0.38	3.8%	1.05	10.5%	1.14	11.4%
15%	0.17	2.5%	0.56	8.4%	0.71	10.7%
20%	0.09	1.8%	0.33	6.7%	0.47	9.4%
25%	0.06	1.4%	0.22	5.4%	0.32	8.1%
30%	0.04	1.1%	0.15	4.4%	0.23	6.9%
35%	0.03	0.9%	0.10	3.7%	0.17	5.9%
40%	0.02	0.7%	0.08	3.0%	0.13	5.0%
45%	0.01	0.6%	0.06	2.5%	0.09	4.3%
50%	0.01	0.5%	0.04	2.1%	0.07	3.6%
55%	0.01	0.4%	0.03	1.8%	0.06	3.0%
60%	0.01	0.3%	0.02	1.4%	0.04	2.5%
65%	0.00	0.3%	0.02	1.2%	0.03	2.1%
70%	0.00	0.2%	0.01	0.9%	0.02	1.7%
75%	0.00	0.2%	0.01	0.7%	0.02	1.3%
80%	0.00	0.1%	0.01	0.6%	0.01	1.0%
85%	0.00	0.1%	0.00	0.4%	0.01	0.7%
90%	0.00	0.1%	0.00	0.3%	0.01	0.5%

Note: For a price increase on N ≥ 2 products, the critical cross elasticity (critical diversion ratio) is compared with the sum of the cross elasticities (diversion ratios) between one product and each of the N-1 other products in the group.

Readers will no doubt notice that the critical values in Tables 1 and 2 are quite different from each other. This shows that the profitability of a particular price increase is quite sensitive to the shape of the demand curve. While unfortunate, since in most cases the shape of the demand curve is unknown, this is unavoidable. It does suggest, however, that one should be cautious in using the critical values in Tables 1 and 2 to evaluate mergers. One way to approach this issue is to view Table 1 as "conservative" in predicting when mergers might be problematic, and to view Table 2 as "conservative" in the opposite sense of stopping mergers that have any chance of being problematic. Alternatively, if one does have information about the shape of the demand curve, the techniques in this article could be used to derive critical cross elasticities and diversion ratios for the profitability of different price increases.[23]

B. Can Critical Loss Analysis Be Consistent with Economic Theory?

Our critique of standard critical loss analysis illustrates how to modify it to make it consistent with static Bertrand oligopoly theory, the most widely-used theory in economics to analyze price competition among imperfectly competitive firms that do not coordinate their pricing. The key predictions of this theory are given in conditions (12) and (13). The important factors for determining the profitability of a price increase are the pre-merger margin and the cross-elasticity of demand or diversion ratio. If the cross elasticity or diversion ratio is less than a critical value that varies inversely with the margin, then the price increase is not profitable.

The standard critical loss formula is an algebraic calculation that is not based on any assumptions about firms' pre-merger behavior. Thus, standard critical loss analysis -- comparing the critical loss formula with evidence about the actual loss -- does not incorporate the consistency requirements of any economic theory. Under most economic theories, higher margins tend to be associated with lower own-price elasticities of demand. The idea is that it only makes sense for a firm to charge high prices (hence high margins) if its customers are not very price sensitive. Standard critical loss analysis effectively ignores this relationship. Therefore, standard critical loss analysis can be consistent with economic theory only in environments in which the usual inverse relationship between margins and own-price elasticities does not hold.

In the introduction, we described four key assumptions of our analysis, at least one of which would have to be violated for standard critical loss analysis to be consistent with

---

[23] Of course, if one knows the shape of the demand curve, one could simulate the *profit-maximizing* post-merger prices to examine the competitive effects of the merger. In our view, this is the best technique for evaluating the competitive effects of a merger.

economic theory. One possibility is that firms fail to pursue profit maximization as their objectives. However, a basic premise of critical loss analysis is that firms *do* evaluate the profitability of a post-merger price increase. Thus, the failure of firms to maximize profits cannot be taken seriously as a justification for conducting standard critical loss analysis.

A second possibility is that firms engage in coordinated pricing prior to the merger, which yields higher margins than implied by the inverse elasticity rule, i.e., $m > 1/E^{Own}$. Pre-merger coordination is certainly a possibility in any merger situation, but standard critical loss analysis still suffers consistency problems in this case. One potential problem is the erroneous conclusion that markets are broad because a hypothetical monopolist who is already charging a monopoly price cannot profitably raise price further. One way to address this problem is by using non-collusive prices as the base for evaluating the profitability of a price increase. However, this places the analysis back into the framework we have developed, in which standard critical loss analysis suffers precisely the consistency problems we have described. A complete investigation of critical loss analysis under coordinated behavior would require an economic theory that permits coordination, predicts the degree of coordination prior the merger, and predicts how the degree of coordination would change with the merger. Such an analysis is beyond the scope of this article. However, it is worth noting that pre-merger coordination is usually viewed as grounds for blocking a merger. The economic logic for this view is that coordination is usually more likely to break down the less concentrated is the industry.

The other potential way that critical loss analysis can be consistent with economic theory is if the increase (decrease) in profits from a small increase in price differs significantly from the decrease (increase) in profits from a small reduction in price. This can occur if the demand or cost curves are kinked.

Consider first the case of kinked demand. If the reduction in quantity from a small price increase exceeds the increase in quantity from a small price decrease, then the firm's own-price elasticity will be higher at prices above the prevailing price than it is at prices below this price. Facing this type of demand, it may pay a profit-maximizing firm to raise price up to the point of the kink, but then not raise price any further. In this situation, the inverse elasticity relationship may not hold, and it is possible that $m > 1/E^{Own}$ (recall E^{Own} is the elasticity defined for an *increase* in price from the prevailing level). If the margin exceeds the inverse of the own-price elasticity at the profit-maximizing price, then the critical cross elasticities and diversion ratios will be higher than the values reported in Tables 1 and 2. Further, for given values of the own- and cross-price elasticities, the higher is the margin, the smaller is the maximum price increase that will be profitable. This is consistent with the prediction of standard critical loss analysis.

A kink in marginal cost can have similar effects. For example, suppose that the merging firms are currently capacity constrained, so that the marginal cost of expanding output is very high, but the cost savings from reducing output are quite low. In this case, the margin earned on the units sold up to capacity can be quite high, potentially higher than the inverse of the own elasticity. As with the kinked demand example, the inverse elasticity relationship may not hold in the short run (until capacity can be adjusted), and higher margins can be consistent with smaller price increases by a hypothetical monopolist.

By focusing on the "standard" cases of smooth demand and costs, we do not mean to suggest that kinked demand or costs would never be important to consider when analyzing the effects of a merger. Economic theory certainly does not rule these cases out. For example, a kinked demand curve may exist for a product if there is a common threshold price above which a significant fraction of customers will substitute to another product or to another firm in a more distant geographic area. On the other hand, if customers are numerous and have heterogeneous preferences, they will substitute to other products at a variety of different prices. In this case the *aggregate* demand across all customers will look relatively smooth because customers will gradually substitute to other products as price is increased.

Kinked costs of the type described above may arise in the short run in some industries in which plants typically operate at capacity and expansion is expensive. On the other hand, if de-bottlenecking can be accomplished in increasing amounts at increasing costs, then the marginal cost curve will look smoother.

Our point is that in one very common case -- smooth demand and cost curves -- the standard critical loss analysis is inconsistent with economic theory, unless firms engage in pre-merger coordination. Our view is that the use of standard critical loss analysis must be accompanied with a credible explanation for why special conditions exist that make the analysis consistent with economic theory. While it is possible that demand or cost curves are kinked at or near the prices that prevail just prior to a merger, an analyst using standard critical loss analysis must provide evidence demonstrating this if the analysis is to be given any weight.

IV. Examples

Standard critical loss analysis has been applied in numerous antitrust cases before the Federal antitrust agencies and in Federal Court. In this section we briefly describe two applications that were conducted in cases that went to trial in U.S. District Court. In each case we show that the conclusions are likely to change when the analysis is made consistent with standard economic theory.

A. Tenet Healthcare

In the *Federal Trade Commission, et al. v. Tenet Healthcare Corporation, et al.* (Tenet Healthcare), two owners of hospitals in the Poplar Bluff, MO area were attempting to merge. Tenet, the acquiring firm, owned one hospital in Poplar Bluff (Lucy Lee) and another hospital (Twin Rivers) within an hour's driving time. Doctor's Regional Medical Center (DRMC), the acquisition target, was a single hospital in Poplar Bluff. In addition, there were four small regional hospitals within an hour's driving time. The merging hospitals provided both primary and secondary care. The smaller hospitals provided only primary care. The FTC claimed that the relevant geographic market included these seven hospitals. The defendant argued that the relevant market included several other hospitals more than a one hour drive from Poplar Bluff, including one very large hospital (over 1000 beds) that was more than three and a half hours driving time from Poplar Bluff.[24]

The defendant's expert report made the argument that because the merging hospitals had very large margins, the percentage of patients they would have to lose to other hospitals to make a price increase unprofitable was not very large. In particular, the report showed that one of the merging hospitals, Lucy Lee, had a margin of 65.9 percent and thus would lose money by increasing price by 5 percent if at least 7.1 percent of its patients switched to another hospital. Based on survey evidence that the expert interpreted as showing that many more than 7.1 percent of patients would switch, the report argued that the existence of high margins made it very unlikely that the merger would result in a price increase. There was nothing in the record to indicate that the expert had presented evidence that the firms were colluding prior to the merger,

---

[24] This information is taken from *FTC and State of Missouri v. Tenet Healthcare et al.*, Preliminary Injunction Decision, U.S. District Court, Eastern District of Missouri, Eastern Division, Filed July 30, 1998, p. 3,4,10, and Expert Report of Barry Harris, Exhibit 5. Driving time was computed using MapQuest.

or that demand or cost curves were kinked at or just above the pre-merger price.

If one uses the information that the margins provide about the willingness of customes to switch, however, the story is likely quite different. Conditions (12) and (13) imply that a 5 percent price increase by both hospitals after the merger would be unprofitable if and only if

$$\frac{.05}{.659(.05+.659)} = .107 > E^{Cross}$$

or

$$\frac{.05}{.05+.659} = .071 > Diversion\ Ratio.$$

That is, a five percent price increase by both hospitals would have been profitable unless the hospitals were not very close substitutes, with a cross elasticity less than .107 and a diversion ratio less than 7.1 percent. This implies that more than 92 percent of the patients at either Lucy Lee or DRMC would have as their second choice some hospital outside of Poplar Bluff instead of the other hospital in Poplar Bluff. This seems unlikely, given that Lucy Lee and DRMC were less than 3 miles apart, while competing hospitals providing both primary and secondary care were over 50 miles away.[25] Thus, it is not surprising that other evidence in the record indicated that the two hospitals in Poplar Bluff were highly competitive. For example, third party payers attributed their success in obtaining discounted rates to "the fierce competition" between the two hospitals.[26]

As is often the case in standard critical loss analysis, the large margins asserted by the defendant's expert were not consistent with testimony about the willingness of customers to switch. In this case, a telephone survey presented by the experts purported to show that many

---

[25] The other Tenet hospital, Twin Rivers, was less than 50 miles away and did provide both primary and secondary care.

patients would switch to other hospitals if faced with a 5 percent price increase. How can this inconsistency be explained or resolved? If we assume that the testimony about the how readily customers would switch products was valid (in this case, the telephone survey), one of five things would have to be true. First, the merging parties might have been over-pricing their product. That is, they might have been able to increase their profits, without a merger, simply by lowering their prices and gaining a large number of new customers. Obviously, since the merging parties provided the testimony about customer substitution, they would have this information after the merger. If they were over-pricing their product at the time of the merger, then one would have expected prices to drop if the merger were blocked. A second possibility is that the pre-merger prices were above the unilateral profit maximizing level because of collusion (explicit or tacit). Since collusion rarely works perfectly forever, one would have expected it to break down at some point if the merger had been blocked, causing prices to drop. With the merger, however, collusion would be easier to enforce, making this price drop less likely. A third possibility is that the defendant's expert mis-measured the margin, i.e., that it was not as high as the expert claimed. This would obviously invalidate the conclusions of the critical loss analysis irrespective of whether they were consistent with standard economic theory. The fourth and fifth possibilities are that the hospital's demand or cost curves were kinked at or near the prevailing price. As mentioned earlier, the expert did not provide evidence of such a kink.

Of course, a distinct possibility is that the testimony about the actual loss from a price increase was not valid. After all, if the parties thought this evidence was reasonable, they would have used it in pricing their products. In fact, when the court examined the telephone survey that formed the basis for the expert's critical loss analysis, it found that its conclusion that a large number of patients would switch hospitals in response to a 5 percent price increase was invalid.

---

[26] Preliminary Injunction Decision, op. cit., p. 6.

By presenting this example we do not intend to suggest that there is no role for testimony about the responsiveness of demand to changes in price. Our point is that such testimony must be reconciled with other evidence, such as that embodied in the firms' margins. Standard critical loss analysis fails to do this.

B. Swedish Match

In *Federal Trade Commission v. Swedish Match North America Inc., et al.*, two producers of loose leaf chewing tobacco were attempting to merge. Experts for the merging firms argued that margins in this industry were quite high, ranging from 55 to 68 percent. As in Tenet Healthcare, the defendant's expert report made the argument that because margins were so high, a significant price increase by a hypothetical monopolist or by the merging firms after the merger was very unlikely. Also like the previous case, the expert report noted that the existence of high margins meant that the amount of sales that would have to be lost to make a five (or ten) percent price increase unprofitable was not very large. The report did not consider the fact that high margins also indicate that the amount of sales lost from a given price increase is likely to be quite small. In fact, in determining the critical loss, the report claimed to be conservative by using the smaller (55 percent) figure for the margin. While this does generate a smaller figure for the critical loss in sales necessary to make a given price increase unprofitable, it also makes it less likely that the actual loss in sales will exceed the critical loss, as we showed above. Thus, using the smaller margin figure is not conservative.

After determining the critical loss for a 5 percent price increase to be 8.3 percent $(=.05/(.05+.55))$, the defendants' expert report then compared this to the actual loss implied by its estimate of the *market* elasticity of demand for loose leaf chewing tobacco.[27] The market demand that was estimated was a smooth curve with no kinks. The market elasticity was estimated to be 2.3, which implied an actual loss from a 5 percent price increase of 10.6 percent.[28] Since the estimated actual loss of 10.6 percent exceeded the critical loss of 8.3 percent, the report claimed to have shown that a 5 percent price increase by a hypothetical monopolist of loose leaf chewing tobacco would be unprofitable. The expert's conclusion was that the relevant product market should include moist snuff in addition to loose leaf chewing tobacco.

The expert's calculation, based on standard critical loss analysis, is mathematically correct. However, the estimated market elasticity is inconsistent with margins as high as the expert claimed. With margins of 55 percent, the elasticity of demand for a single brand would be 1.82 (1/.55=1.82) if prices were chosen unilaterally prior to the merger. If the margin were higher, the elasticity would have to be even smaller. Since the elasticity of demand for the whole market must be less than the elasticity of demand for a single brand, the claimed market demand elasticity of 2.3 is inconsistent with profit maximization.[29]

Again, this example is not meant to disparage the use of demand estimation for defining markets and/or assessing market power in antitrust investigations. Our point is that econometric estimates of demand elasticities must be consistent with other evidence about substitution, such as that implied by margins. One cannot simultaneously claim that demand is very elastic for the

---

[27] The experts actually couched their analysis in terms of the critical elasticity above which a price increase would not be profitable. This analysis is mathematically equivalent to examining the critical loss above which a price increase would not be profitable.

[28] The estimated elasticity of 2.3 is a point elasticity, not an arc elasticity. Under constant elasticity demand (assumed by the expert), this implies that a five percent price increase will cause a 10.6 percent loss in sales. One can use the formulas in footnote 23 to verify this.

[29] The court did not rely on the econometric analysis of the parties in reaching its conclusion in this case.

purposes of estimating lost sales from a price increase and that margins are very high, requiring that demand must be very inelastic.

We explained above that in addition to margins, the cross elasticities of demand among the merging firms' brands are critical for evaluating the profitability of a post-merger price increase. The defendant's expert report in Swedish Match did not provide estimates of the cross-elasticities among loose-leaf brands. However, it did present an estimate of the cross-elasticity of demand for *all* loose leaf chewing tobacco with respect to a price index for all moist snuff. This cross elasticity was estimated to be .5. Given this much substitution between two *different* types of smokeless tobacco --- loose leaf chewing tobacco and moist snuff --- it seems likely that the amount of substitution between the two leading brands of loose leaf chewing tobacco would also be significant. By using equation (12), however, one can see that the cross-elasticity between the two brands would have to be much smaller than the cross elasticity between loose-leaf and moist snuff to make a post-merger price increase of 5 percent unprofitable:

$$\frac{.05}{.55(.05+.55)} = .152 > E^{Cross}.$$

So, unless the cross elasticity between two different types of smokeless tobacco is more than three times greater than the cross elasticity between the two leading brands of one type of smokeless tobacco (loose-leaf), the defendant's own econometric analysis suggested that the merging firms would have found a 5 percent price increase to be profitable post-merger.

V. Conclusion

We have shown that the inference typically drawn from critical loss analysis --- that high margins make a merger less likely to be anticompetitive --- is often inconsistent with economic theory. Firms set their margins to maximize their profits. The more close substitutes there are for a firm's product, the lower the firm's margin must be to prevent customers from switching to those products. Conversely, the fewer the number of close substitutes a firm faces, the higher the margin will be. Thus, when two or more substitutes come under common ownership, the degree to which competition is reduced (loosely speaking) is greater when margins are high (because there is less competition to begin with) than when margins are low. Therefore, it should not be surprising that economic theory predicts that mergers tend to lead to greater, not smaller, price increases when margins are high rather than when margins are low. Conversely, theory predicts that mergers in more competitive markets (those with lower margins) are less likely to cause significant price increases than mergers in less competitive markets (those with higher margins), contrary to what critical loss analysis purports to show. In summary, it is the approach of the Merger Guidelines (mergers in concentrated markets are more likely to be anticompetitive) that is consistent with economic theory, not critical loss analysis as it is typically practiced.

Where does this leave critical loss analysis as tool in antitrust practice? In our opinion, critical loss analysis has led to enormous confusion about the economic factors that govern firms' pricing incentives. The technique has been mis-used so frequently that arguments that are inconsistent with basic economic theory have almost gained a measure of legitimacy in antitrust cases. It is now common for people to assume that high pre-merger margins imply broader markets and/or a smaller likelihood of anticompetitive effects. This article has shown that this assumption is not correct because it is generally not consistent with basic economic theory.